JOURNEY TO EGYPT
COLORING & ACTIVITY BOOK

I0189910

The Great Adventures of

Ishaq
& Kadeedee

JOURNEY TO EGYPT COLORING & ACTIVITY BOOK
The Great Adventures of Ishaq & Kadeedee Activity Book Series

Published by ILLUMINATION PRESS
ATLANTA, GA

ISBN: 978-1-950681-11-2

Illustrated by Dwight Pitts II

QUANTITY PURCHASES: Schools, companies, professional groups, clubs, and other organizations may qualify for special terms when ordering quantities of this title. For information, email authors@inspirationalaurhors.com.

ILLUMINATION PRESS
c/o Benecia Ponder
1100 Peachtree Street
Suite 250
Atlanta, GA 30309
InspirationalAuthors.com

The Great Adventures of
Ishaq
& Kadeedee
JOURNEY TO EGYPT

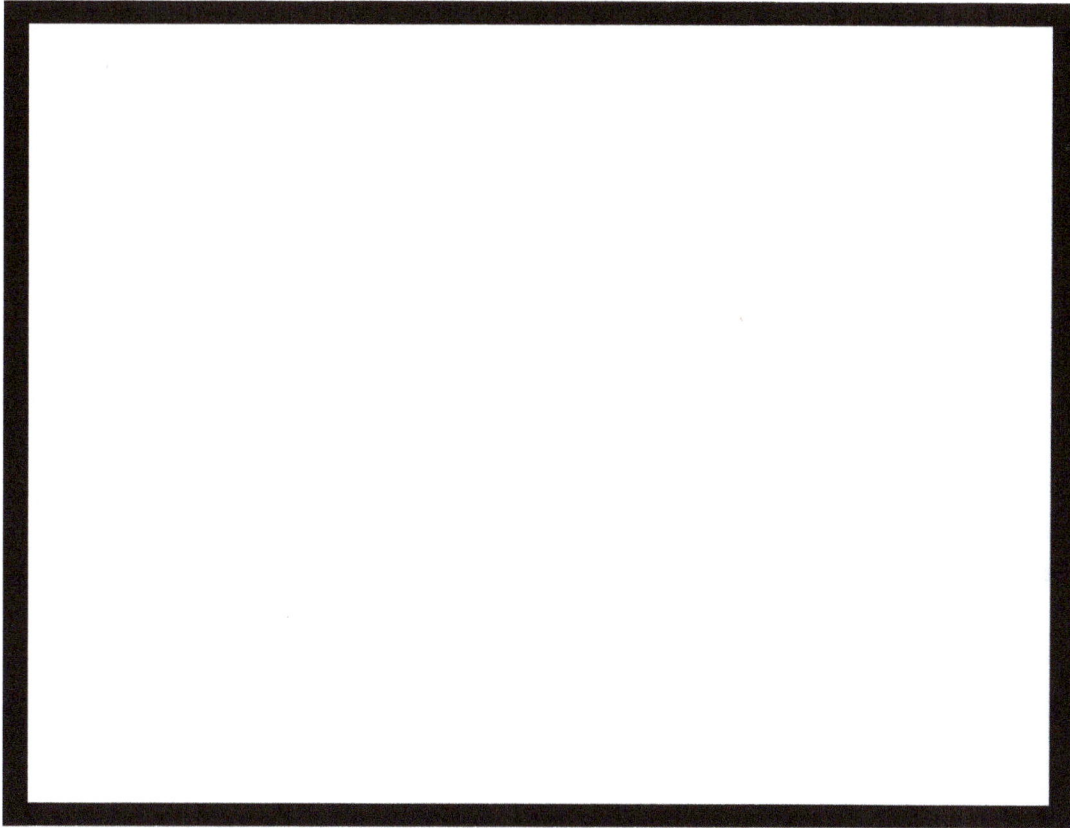

This Adventure Pack belongs to

_____

EGYPT

WELCOME TO EGYPT

MADE IN -EGYPT-

WE'RE GOING TO EGYPT

ADVENTURE

1 - red
2 - blue
3 - gray

EGYPT

Complete the Maze

Help the Adventure Jet travel to Egypt.

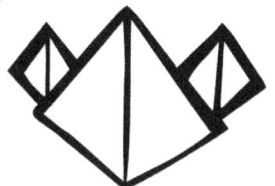

Find your way through the tangles.

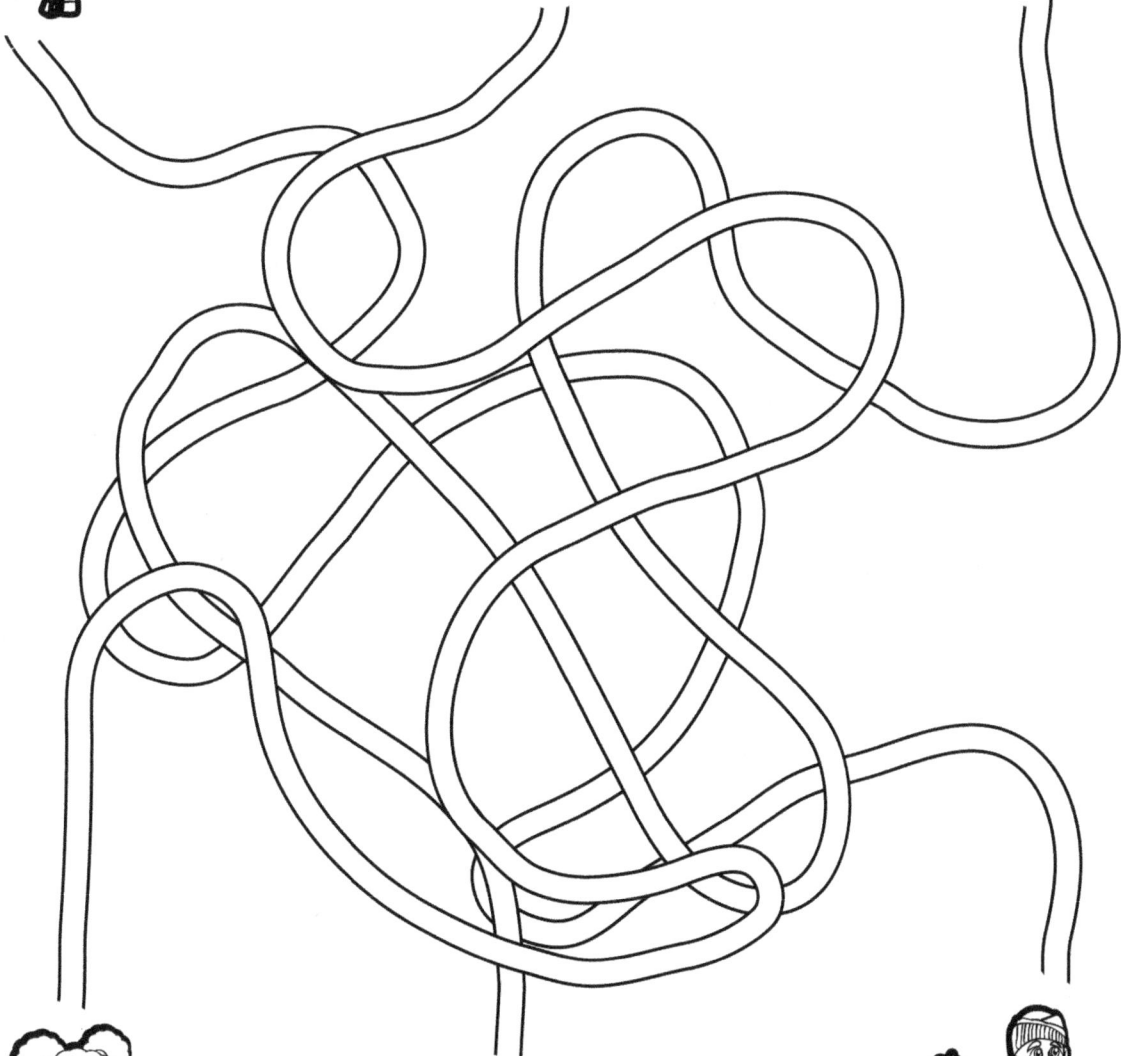

Connect the dots

Match the picture and words

pyramid

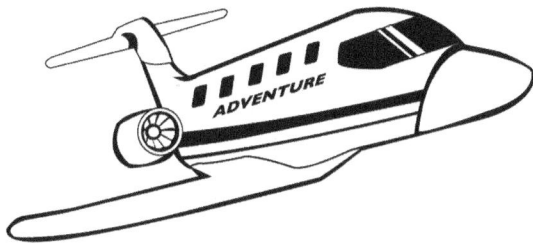

camel

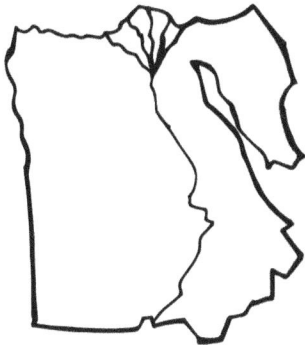

Sphinx

Egypt

jet

Match the picture and words

Hieroglyphics

lotus

eagle

mummy

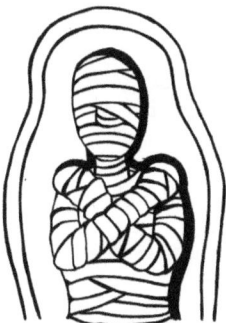

flag

**National Bird of Egypt
Golden Eagle**

Flag of Egypt

| 1 | 3 | 2 |

1 - red   2 - black   3 - yellow/gold

Which one is different?

Which one is different?

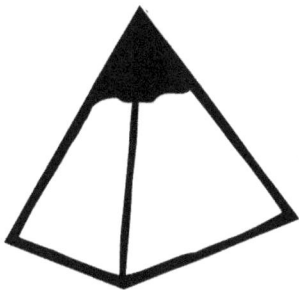

KING TUT

QUEEN NEFERTITI

Find the shadow

I Spy Count and Write

Word Search

```
D N E F E R T I T I
V A F A I E E S F T
P W D T U T G P Y I
Y Z I V P G Y H Y S
R U C C E M P I Z H
A F A R X N T N Y A
M Z M T C V T X S Q
I B E T K L Q U M L
D V L T X M U Y R V
L K A D E E D E E E
```

Adventure   Nefertiti   Pyramid   Kadeedee

Sphinx   Camel   Tut   Ishaq

Egypt

Draw the camel step by step

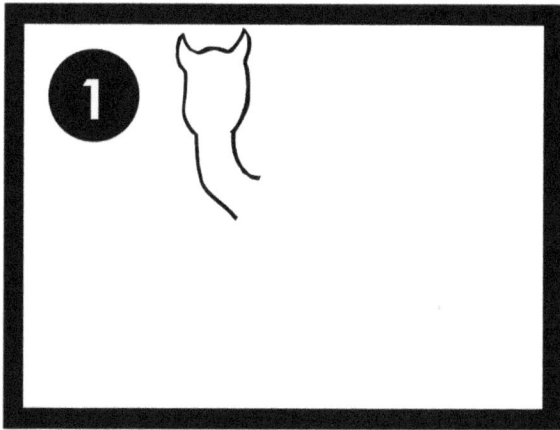

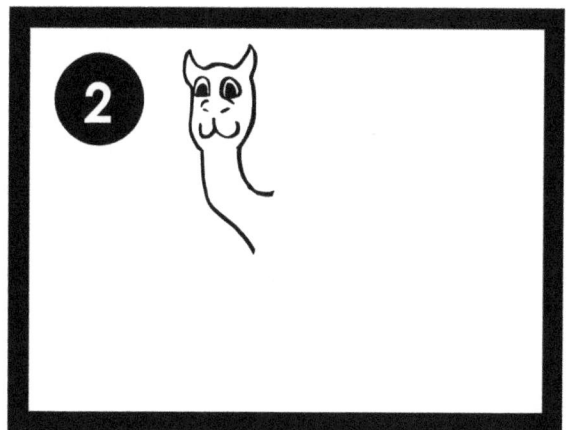

Camels can live for about 40 years.
Camels can run as fast as 65 kilometers per hour
and sustain a walking speed of 40 kilometers per hour.

HIEROGLYPHIC

ALPHABET

 A
 A I Y
 AH
 B

 C K
 CC KH
 CH TH
 D

 E Y
 E I
 F PH V
 G

 G J
 H
 L
 M

 N
 O
 P
 QU

 R
 S C
 SH
 T

 U W Oo
 U Y
 X
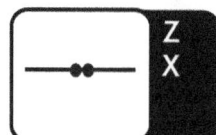 Z X

ADVENTURE PACK

Crack the code

Write Your Name in Hieroglyphics

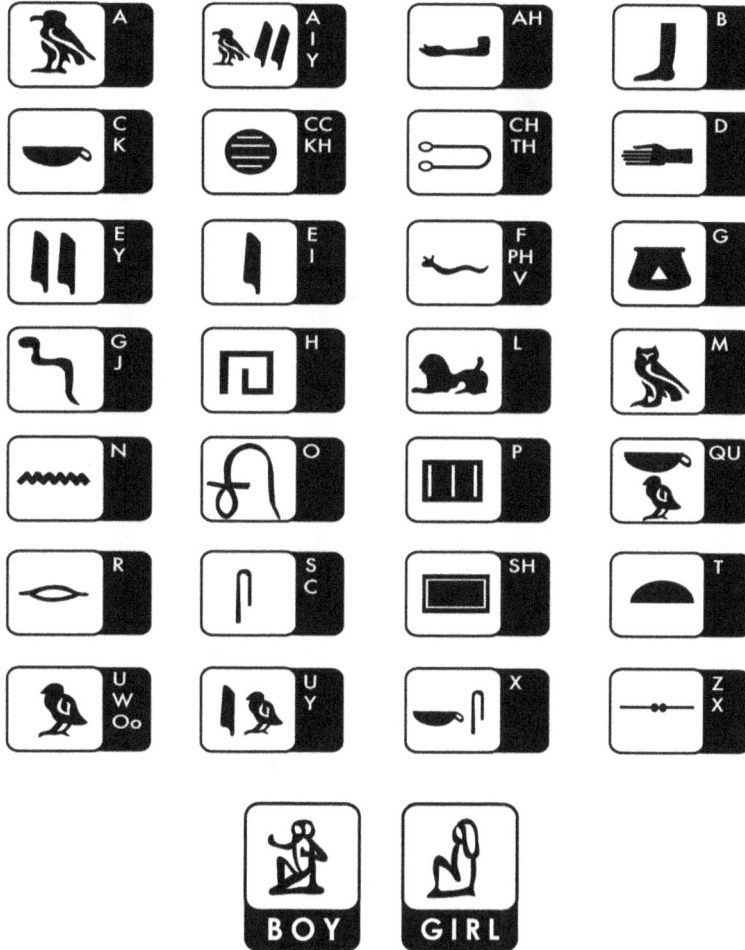

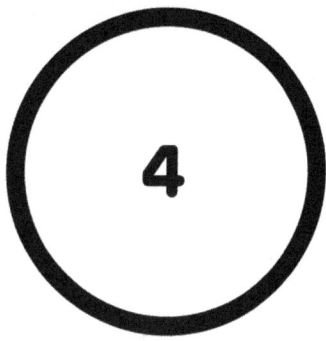

4

1

2

2

2

2

2

2

3

2

2

2

2

2

2

2

2

2

1 - blue
2 - green
3- brown
4- yellow

1

ADVENTURE PACK
ADVENTURE PACK
HIEROGLYPHIC
ALPHABET
ADVENTURE PACK

www.ingramcontent.com/pod-product-compliance
Lightning Source LLC
Chambersburg PA
CBHW081226020426
42331CB00012B/3085